Rec'd from R.B
on 3-13-25

CHARLEY WEAVER'S
Letters from Mamma

By CLIFF ARQUETTE

With introduction by Jack Paar

From coast to coast more people are keeping their television sets on much later, more nights because of Cliff Arquette.

A regular on NBC's "*Jack Paar Show*," Cliff's meteoric rise to fame among late evening watchers is the result of his portrayal of a likable old codger Charley Weaver, who hails from Mount Idy, and who reads side-splitting letters from his "Mamma."

These letters are a complete report on the doin's in the old home town. Through the magic of television, and now the pages of this book, Charley's "Mamma" has made real people out of Birdie Rodd, Grandpa Ogg, Elsie Krack, Dr. Beemish and all the others. Real people and normal people. Normal except that the darndest things happen to them!

As Jack Paar says, "Charley Weaver is a witch. He knows more about comedy than anyone alive, which he isn't.... Old Charley not only gets laughs on a Monday night but he gets them all during Lent... even when we are playing to a convention of Martian undertakers who have just heard bad news. That's witchcraft!"

This book proves Jack Paar's point.

NBC Photographs by Robert S. Ganley.

THE JOHN C. WINSTON COMPANY
Philadelphia • Toronto

CHARLEY WEAVER'S
LETTERS
from
MAMMA

CHARLEY WEAVER'S

LETTERS from MAMMA

by CLIFF ARQUETTE

INTRODUCTION BY JACK PAAR

Illustrated by Sidney A. Quinn
(With a Little Help from Charley)

The John C. Winston Company
Philadelphia • Toronto

© 1959 by
CLIFF ARQUETTE

FIRST EDITION

The Library of Congress catalog entry for this
book appears at the end of the text.

Made in the United States of America

Introduction by Jack Paar

CHARLEY WEAVER is a witch. He knows more about comedy than anyone alive—which he isn't. On the "Tonight" show, the most difficult time to get laughs from a studio audience is on Monday night. I don't know why. It has something to do with everybody doing the washing and laundry—and most people know that our theater audience is made up of Chinese. Old Charley not only gets laughs on a Monday night, but he gets them all during Lent . . . in the rain . . . even when we are playing to a convention of Martian undertakers who have just heard bad news. That's witchcraft!

Inside those glassless glasses, you will find two of the bluest, kindest eyes a witch could have. And I have never seen Charley on or off stage without a smile. It's like having a Mona Lisa who drinks as your friend. When I am blue or depressed, I have only to look at his smile to feel better. And his smile is not put on with make-up—although I suspect he puts a rubber band over his lips and hooks the ends over his ears.

Sometimes his jokes are old, and I live in the constant fear that the audience will beat him to the punch line, but they never have. And I suspect that if they ever do, he will rewrite the ending on the spot. I would not like to say that all his jokes are old, although some have been found carved in stone. What I want to say is that in a free-for-all ad lib session, Charley Weaver has and will beat the fastest gun alive.

Charley Weaver has done more for the success of the "Tonight" show than anyone who was ever on it. He is my "wild old man," and it's understandable, when you realize that before every show he rinses his jockey shorts in turpentine. Nobody will ever catch him.

JACK PAAR

Letters from Mamma

Dear Mickey: *(Mamma always used to say, are you a man or a mouse?)* Things are fine in Mount Idy *(she goes on).* Everybody in Mount Idy is celebrating Halloween. Elsie Krack dropped in last night for a minute and got a ticket for double-parking her broom. Then she got another one, when she went home, for flying without a pilot's license.

Your father and I went to a Halloween party at Wallace Swine's house last night. Your father glued a keyhole over his eye and went as a Peeping Tom. I went as Little Bo Peep. My, the car was crowded with all those sheep. During the party they had to give Grandpa Ogg artificial respiration. He was bobbing for apples and his beard got waterlogged.

Clara Kimball Moots got first prize for having the ugliest false face. She had to give the prize back, though, because at twelve o'clock when everybody took his mask off, we found out she wasn't wearing one.

Later, we all went over to Grandma Ogg's to watch television on her glasses. You see, Grandma was a nurse at that recent unpleasantness at Gettysburg, and she forgot to duck. They had to put a steel plate in her head. One day, not too long ago, she was out in the field plowing when a thunderstorm came up, and Grandma was struck on her steel plate by a bolt of lightning. Ever since then she can get television on her glasses. You can see Ozzie on one side and Harriet on the other. Well, we didn't get to see any shows. Some smart kids had soaped her glasses.

Well, son, I must close now and go help your father. He was out Trick or Treating. I just happened to catch him with a cute little trick, and now they're treating him at the General Hospital.

Love,
Mamma

Dear Sargeant Friday: *(Mamma always said I'd do in a pinch.)* Things are fine in Mount Idy *(she goes on).* Ludlow Bean volunteered to go up to the moon in a rocket, but they turned him down; seems they don't make a two-headed space suit. Ludlow's always getting into trouble. Last night a policeman stopped him on the street and asked him if he had been playing poker. Ludlow said no, but he had just left three guys who had.

Doctor Beemish was caught driving while intoxicated the other night; they let him go, though, as he was already late for an operation.

Son, I seen you on the television the other night with Goo Goo Schultz. I know her real well. In fact, I know her so well I just call her by her first name—Goo!

I knew her when she didn't know where her next millionaire was coming from.

I ran into her once when she just got back from Europe. I said to her, "Goo," I said, "did you see the white cliffs of Dover?" And she said, "See them! I had dinner with them!" Oh, my, she does meet the nicest people. Your father and I went over to Grandma Ogg's last night to watch television on her glasses.

We didn't get to see any shows, though, 'cause she's so absent-minded she never remembers where she leaves her glasses after she empties them.

Well, son, I must close now and go help your father. He's been petting a little kitten outside. It has a white stripe down its back . . . yes! . . . to high heaven!

Love,
Mamma

Dear Plymouth Rock: *(Mamma always said I was chicken.)* Things are fine in Mount Idy *(she goes on)*. Well, sir, the schools have started, and Grandpa Ogg is in the fifth grade. They can't put him in the sixth because his father's still there.

It's so cute to see Grandpa goin' to school, rollin' a hoop—of course it's around a barrel. When they told him he was in the fifth, he misunderstood and thought they said, "Bring a fifth."

Leonard Box and Elsie Krack broke their engagement. After going steady for twelve years, they got married. We were all surprised. Elsie is so ugly, you know, she's been turned down more times than a bedspread. Her teeth stick out so far in front she can eat an apple through a picket fence. She once bit, Elsie Loves Clyde, into an oak tree. When your father asked her how it felt to have buck teeth, she got real mad. She said, "I'll have you understand these teeth cost me *six* bucks!"

You know, son, it's all right to be ugly, but she overdoes it. Two weeks ago she won first prize in a beauty contest—it was for mules.

Leonard is a traveling salesman now and he takes her on every trip he makes. He says she's so ugly, he'd rather do that than kiss her good-by!

Well, son, I must close now and go help your father. He just lit a match to see if there was any gasoline in the gas tank—there was!

Love,
Mamma

Dear Peyton: *(Mamma always wanted me to have my own place!)* Things are fine in Mount Idy *(she goes on)*. Somebody gave your father a tuxedo, and as soon as he learns to stay up half the night and drink out of a bottle, he's going to become a musician. He's taken up the trombone. He took it up while the store clerk wasn't looking.

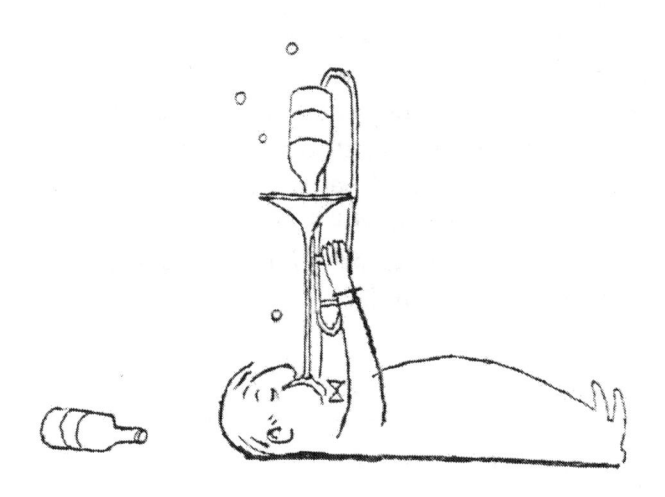

The other day he was practicing, and the man next door came over and said, "Do you know there's a little old lady sick over there?" and your father said, "No—but if you'll hum a few bars of it, I'll fake it for you!"

Then the man said, "Do you know 'The Road to Mandalay?'" and your father said, "Yes, shall I play it?" and the man said, "No—*take* it!" Yesterday I got the nicest postcard from your father, from somewhere east of Suez.

I just had a big fight with your grandfather. He's so changeable. Monday he wanted beans, Tuesday he wanted beans, Wednesday he wanted beans, and here it is Thursday and all of a sudden he doesn't want beans. He wants bean soup.

I've never seen anyone eat like your grandfather. Most people use a knife and fork. He eats as if food were going out of style. He'll eat anything but bananas. He says bananas are a waste of time. After you skin them and throw the bone away, there's nothing left to eat.

Well, son, I must close now and go help your grandfather. I think he's choking to death. He was eating a piece of horse meat and somebody said, whoa!

       Love,
       Mamma

Dear Steinway: *(Mamma always wanted me to be upright and grand.)* Things are fine in Mount Idy *(she goes on)*. As you remember, son, ever since Grandma Ogg was struck by lightning she can get television on her glasses. Yesterday, your father and I went over to Grandma's house to watch the baseball game on her glasses. We was that disappointed! Grandma has the hay fever so bad the game was rained out. The creeping nussman* is bad this time of year.

Your father told Grandma carrots are good for the eyes, so she promised to eat a bunch every day so we can enjoy Perry Como next week. I was afraid if she ate too many carrots she might get rabbit ears, but your father says that's even better—she'll get much better reception. We saw Elsie Krack the other day, which made us all very happy, because when you see Elsie at this time of the year it means six weeks of

---

* Not to be confused with Armenian trailing nussman.

good weather. We found out the State Department is sending her to West Berlin. They want one thing there that the Russians can't copy. Elsie is going to write a book about her trip, entitled, *A Broad Broad, Abroad*. It should be a smash. We all hate to see her go. We'll miss her carefree swinging through the trees.

Incidentally, your father is very sad today. He just lost five thousand dollars. The price of hogs went **up** and he didn't have a one.

Well, son, I must close now and go help **your** father. He just tried to give a mule a hot-foot.

Love,
Mamma

Dear Harry James: *(Mamma always said I should toot my own horn.)* Things are fine in Mount Idy *(she goes on)*. Elsie Krack was just married, so yesterday we all pitched in and gave her a shower. It took six of us to drag her into the bathroom. She didn't mind the strong soap, but she did squawk a little about the steel wool.

My, she got some lovely gifts! Mrs. Bean gave her a box of wet facial tissue for making instant spitballs. Mrs. Swine gave her a gift certificate for an eight-by-ten-foot hole, to be dug anywhere in the United States. Your father and I gave her a lovely old Indian blanket that comes complete with a lovely old Indian —name sex preferred—and Clara Kimball Moots's little girl gave her the German measles.

Then we all sat down to a lovely dinner of champagne and French toast served by an adorable little Eskimo girl with one tooth, named Ockluck. I don't know what the name of her other tooth was. Then for dessert we had windmill pudding. Windmill pudding is the kind that you'll get some if it goes around.

The prospective bridegroom was there, and after dinner he didn't open his mouth all evening. By mistake he picked up the glue bottle instead of the maple syrup for his French toast.

Well, son, I must close now and go help your father. He just stuck his finger into a turtle's mouth to see if it was a snapping turtle. It was.

                        Love,
                        Mamma

Dear Simian: *(Mamma always said I was a cute little monkey.)* Things are fine in Mount Idy *(she goes on)*. Ludlow Bean was arrested the other day for stealing a woman's change purse. He told the judge that he hadn't been feeling well, and he thought the change would do him good. He says he hopes they won't throw the book at him because he never learned to read. He says he's going to plead insanity because he's nuts about the new jail. He likes his cell because it has a southern exposure—there are two Confederate prisoners in the next cell.

Too bad he's in jail. He was doing so well. His race horse won so much money last year, the horse finally bought a string of people.

Will you ever forget the time Ludlow fell into the hay bailer, and from then on had to have all of his clothes made square? We're all proud of Ludlow. When he first came to Mount Idy, he started out in a small way. He started as an organ grinder, with one small monkey. He worked hard and saved. Two years later he expanded—now he has a pipe organ and a gorilla. He doesn't have any trouble with people putting money in the cup now.

Well, son, I must close now and go help your father carry a two hundred-pound sack of sugar up into the woods. I don't know what he's cookin' up there, but you never seen a happier bunch of birds and squirrels in your life.

Love,
Mamma

Dear Virginia: *(Mamma always said I was a ham.)* Things are fine in Mount Idy *(she goes on)*. Your father went to the dentist today to have two teeth extracted—from his leg. He also had to have Wallace Swine's little boy extracted. The doctor asked your father if he wanted gas, and he said, "Yes, and you'd better check my oil, too!" Then the doctor explained that it was laughing gas, and your father said, "Go ahead and pull them all out. I'll do anything for a laugh!" Then he said, "How long will I keep laughing, Doc?" and the doctor said, "Right up to the minute you get your bill."

Today your father said to me, "Honey, I'm homesick." And I said, "But dear, this *is* your home!" and he said, "I know it—but I'm sick of it!"

If he keeps that up, I'll *dig* him a home. Ha ha!

Yesterday was our natal day, we had boiled natals for supper. We also exchanged presents. He exchanged the one I gave him, and I exchanged the one he gave me. He gave me a washing machine, but it wasn't any good. The paddles kept knocking my hat off. I gave him a lovely bathrobe, but the colors ran when he took a bath in it.

Well, son, I must close now and go help your father. He just threw a boomerang and now he's lying out on the front lawn, real still. You know—those things really *do* come back.

                                      Love,
                                      Mamma

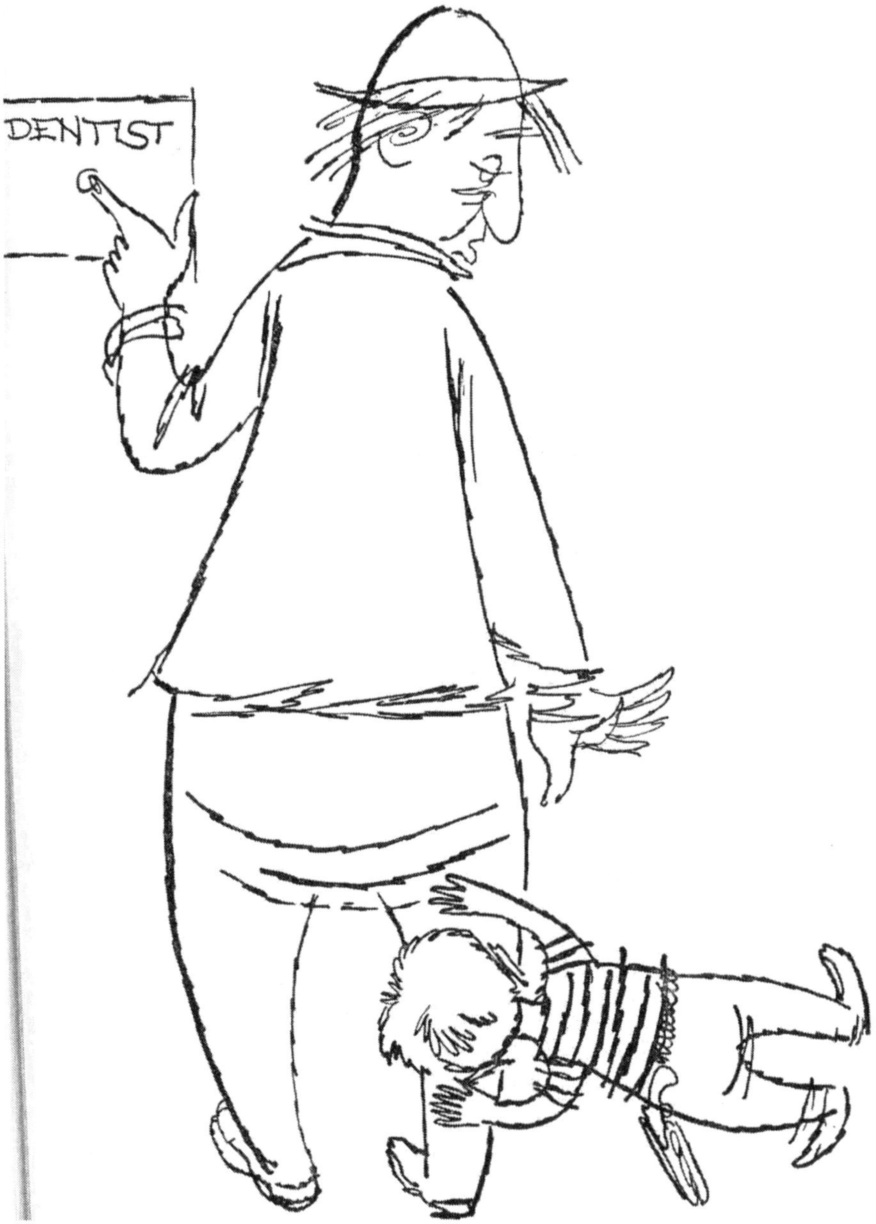
DENTIST

Dear Perry: *(Mamma always wanted me to be real relaxed.)* Things are fine in Mount Idy *(she goes on).* Clara Kimball Moots gave a fashion show yesterday. It was held in Wallace Swine's Pool and Billiard Parlor. One of the models, Goo Goo Schultz (no relation to Goo Goo Finchley), wore a new chemise dress, cut very low in front and back. Clara stepped up to the microphone and explained that this dress was to be worn to teas. Byron Ogg, who got in on a pass, hollered, "To tease who?" He should be out of the hospital in a month or two.

The sack dress is finally becoming very popular in Mount Idy. Clara showed some that had built-in potatoes—I think!

Old Grandma Heise, the richest woman in Mount Idy, passed away last week and they found thirty thousand dollars hidden in her bustle. Your father said, "That's an awful lot of money to leave behind!"

Your father ain't well, son. He wanted to crack some walnuts yesterday, but we didn't have any, so he spent most of the day on the front porch, cracking his knuckles. He didn't want the neighbors to think we couldn't afford them. I later cracked him on the head.

Somebody's pet peacock got into our chicken yard the other day, and it was the first one your father ever seen. He come rushin' into the house and said, "What do you think? One of our chickens is in bloom!" Yes, son, he's real sick.

We're having a lot of trouble with two of our chickens. They get at either end of the chicken yard, then run at each other as fast as they can, just barely missing each other. I guess they must be playing People. It's like I've always said, "It's an ill wind—that blows from the stockyards."

       Love,
       Mamma

Dear Quincy: *(Mamma always said I was a pain in the neck.)* Things are fine in Mount Idy *(she goes on).* Your father and I spent Sunday with Wallace Swine and his family. My, but their oldest boy is spoiled—a steam roller ran over him. His father put a stamp on him and mailed him to the Mayo brothers. He's coming along fine now. They have to put a bookmark in bed with him, though, to find him. Byron Ogg says as soon as the kite-flying season comes in they can put a string on him and fly him back to Mount Idy.

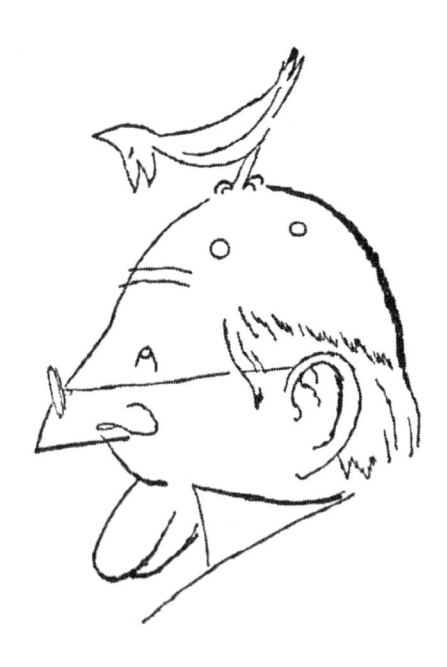

Grandpa Snider was rushed to the hospital suffering from 324 holes in his head. He explained, later, that Monday night as he left work he was attacked by a flock of woodpeckers. It seems that when he left his job at the Mount Idy sawmill that fateful night, he forgot to dust the sawdust out of his hair. We're all happy the vicious birds didn't know Grandpa has a wooden leg.

Your own Grandpa Weaver has been giving us at home a lot of trouble lately. About every ten minutes he grabs his air raid warden's helmet and rushes outside, blowing his whistle and hollering, "Head for the shelter—enemy bombers!" Nobody's got the heart to tell him a bunch of wasps built a nest in his ear trumpet.

The entire population of Mount Idy—308 souls in all—was rushed to the Mount Idy Emergency Hospital on Memorial Day, due to a slight oversight on the part of Ludlow Bean. At noon, the old Civil War cannon in the town square was fired, and everybody in town rushed out to the park and dove into our new swimming pool. Ludlow Bean was the only one who didn't go to the hospital. He was also the one who forgot to fill the pool.

Love,
Mamma

Dear Elsa: *(Mamma always wanted me to be the life of the party.)* Things are fine in Mount Idy *(she goes on)*—all except the crops. As our corn is only an inch high, the birds have to kneel down to eat it. Our wheat is so short your father's going to have to lather it before he can mow it. Also, your father sold our horse and he wants to buy a cow. I want him to buy a tractor. I told him he'd look awful silly trying to ride a cow, and he said he'd look a lot sillier tryin' to milk a tractor. On second thought, knowing your father, I don't think he would.

Anyway, we already have a cow. She's very friendly. She'll let anyone milk her—even people with cold hands.

Leonard Box had all the horns removed from his cows. He said it was cheaper to do that than join the musicians' union.

Gomar Cool finally got engaged. He met this girl in a revolving door, and they started going around together. Her father recently died and left her everything. They don't know how much it is because they haven't gone through his pants pockets yet. She's the prettiest girl in Mount Idy. She reminds you of the Loch Ness monster—if it were taller. Gomar tried to get her a twenty-four-carat diamond, but nobody would swap him a diamond for twenty-four carrots. He was even willing to throw in an eggplant and a watermelon.

The other day when Gomar was taking a load of hay to town, his wagon hit a rut and the whole load overturned on the road. A farmer came out and invited Gomar in to dinner. Gomar said, "I better not, Father wouldn't like it." The farmer insisted, so in he went and had a wonderful dinner. After dinner they played the Gramophone, looked at the family album, played several games of Parchesi. Then Gomar thanked the farmer and said, "I guess Father wouldn't like my being here." The farmer said, "Where is your father?" and Gomar says, "He's under the hay!"

                Love,
                Mamma

Dear Ida: *(Mamma always wanted me to be as sweet as apple cider.* Mamma ain't been the same since the baby came.) Things are fine in Mount Idy *(she goes on).* Grandpa Snider just got home from entertaining the troops. Of all the outfits he played for, he said he was best received by General Grant's men. My, he's aged so since he left here. They finally had to arrest him. Every time he'd hear an auto backfire, he'd grab his musket and shoot a mailman. He saw his first movie the other night. It was a Civil War picture. During the battle scene he lay down in the aisle with his musket, picked off two ushers, and put twenty-seven holes in the picture screen. The sheriff grabbed him when he rushed to the candy counter and demanded a package of Minié balls and a case of hardtack.

Elsie Krack arrived back in town yesterday. You remember, son, she left town two weeks ago by rail. Leonard Box and Byron Ogg were carrying the rail. Everyone in town is worried about Elsie. She swallowed a whistle. Now every time she sneezes, she whistles. Also, her hay fever is very bad now. She's been sneezing so much lately that she doesn't know what to do with the pack of forty dogs that keeps following her around. Yesterday she sneezed so hard everybody in town went home to lunch.

Birdie Rodd is pretty upset. Saturday night somebody broke into her house and stole her bathtub. She says whoever did it can keep the washrag, soap and the tub, but she would like them to return her mother.

Well, son, I must close now and go help your father. He was cranking our old car and forgot to take it out of gear. Son, how do you get tire marks off a person's forehead?

Love,
Mamma

Dear Sputnik: *(Mamma used to say I was always up in the air—for no good reason at all.)* Things are fine in Mount Idy *(she goes on)*. Grandpa Ogg dropped by yesterday. My, he's getting so nearsighted. He showed us a cane he picked up on the way over. It rattled twice and bit your father. Later, the snake died.

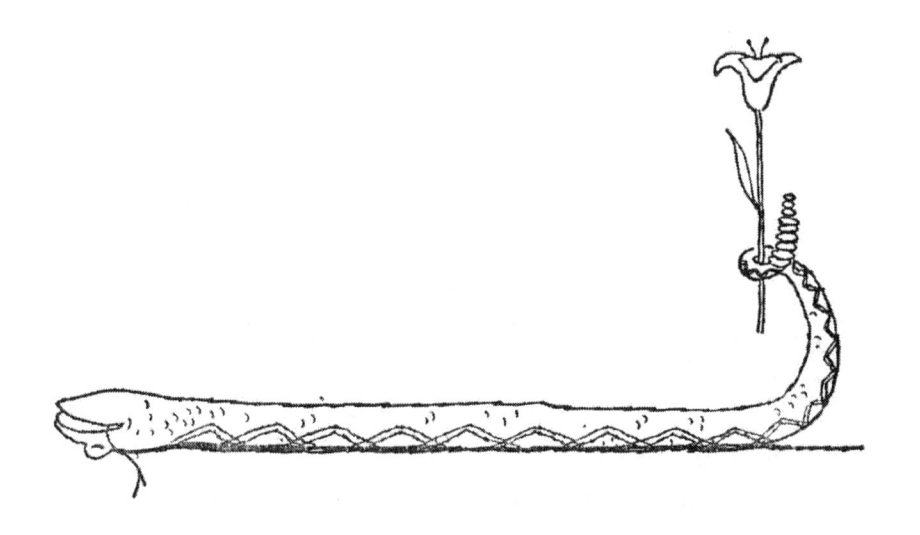

Grandpa is a war veteran. He fought with General Lee, then he fought with General Pershing, and, last, he fought with General Eisenhower. Grandpa just can't get along with anybody.

He told us it was Grandma Ogg's birthday. Your father says, "What you gonna get for her?" and Grandpa says, "I figger a dollar and a quarter if I throw in a bushel of peaches!"

Then your father got out the checkerboard. My, it was exciting. First Grandpa jumped your father—then your father jumped Grandpa—then Grandpa jumped your father again, then I stepped in and I said, "You two cut that out and sit down and play checkers!" Ha-ha! After the checker game your father drove Grandpa home. He had to use a chair and a whip to do it, though. Grandpa got pretty mad at your father. Once he stopped and turned around and put his fist right in your father's face, and he says, "You see this fist?" And your father says, "Yes, I see it." Grandpa says, "What would you do if you had a fist like this?" and your father says, "I'd wash it!" Then your father got up off the ground.

Well, son, I must close now and go help your father. He and Byron Ogg were having a contest to see who could lean out of the attic window the farthest. You guessed it—your father won.

                                          Love,
                                        Mamma

Dear Rocket: *(Mamma always wanted me to leave my pad and take off.)* Things are fine in Mount Idy *(she goes on)*. Your father is going to the dentist to have his head extracted. He got it caught in a public mailbox yesterday. You know, son, how your father loves to read.

Elsie Krack was in a beauty contest that was run by her father and seven brothers, and she won first prize. We was all amazed. For a while we thought her father was going to win it. Elsie looked lovely in a red Bikini bathing suit and she painted her toenails red—all twelve of them. Her hair was done in a very pretty upsweep with tiny ringlets of curls all around her bald spot. She's already had an offer to star in a Hollywood movie. It's called, *How to Clean a Septic Tank*. Probably a war picture.

Grandma Ogg had to go to the doctor and he told her to drink a glass of huckleberry wine after a hot bath. However, she never got to the wine—she couldn't finish drinking the hot bath.

Then I saw her yesterday and she had a rope, and she was going down the sidewalk, skipping like mad. So I says, "What you doin', Grandma?" and she says, "Well, the doctor give me some pills and told me to take them for two days, then skip a day!" Poor old soul was just about worn out.

Well, son, I've got to close now and go help your father. He's been up on a ladder painting the chimney, and he just stepped back to admire his work.

       Love,
       Mamma

Dear Giblets: *(Mamma always said I'd wind up in a stew.)* Things are fine in Mount Idy *(she goes on)*. Birdie Rodd got married yesterday. My, it was a lovely wedding. Just as she started to walk down the aisle all the lights went out. That didn't stop Birdie—she kept right on going. She knew the way by heart. Birdie gets married so often she keeps her bridesmaids, ushers and flower girls on salary.

Ludlow Bean, the groom, got pretty badly banged up at the wedding. Somebody hit him with some rice. It was still in the fifty-pound bag. Later, for a joke, they tied his shoes to the back axle of the car. It wasn't until eighty-two miles later Birdie noticed Ludlow was still in them. He thought it was a good joke, and he was still laughing when they wheeled him into surgery. Rather hysterically, though. As soon as he's better, they're going to have a party for him. That party is the sheriff of Adams County. He's going to arrest Ludlow for erasing eighty-two miles of white line down the center of the turnpike.

Birdie got some lovely wedding presents. Her new mother- and father-in-law gave her a one-way ticket to Devil's Island, her new husband gave her a black eye, and she was severely bitten by a pack of small boys in the church parking lot. They scattered when she tore a fender off her car and advanced upon them.

Well, son, I must close now and go help your father. He just got his ear caught in the wringer.

Love,
Mamma

Dear Elberta: *(Mamma always said I was a peach.)* Things are fine in Mount Idy *(she goes on)*. Elsie Krack is very happy. They've put up her picture in the post office. She says it's nice to be wanted. She's had a little trouble with the law. She picked up a new hubcap the other day. The car was still on it. They are going to charge her with kidnaping. There were several goats with their kids in the back seat at the time.

Elsie's not afraid. She says, "Stone walls do not a prison make!" and your father says, "No, but they sure help!" Ha-ha.

Your big fat Uncle Harvey gave your father a pig for his birthday, and I said, "Ain't that jest like Harvey?" And your father says, "No—I think Harvey's a little fatter!"

Our old horse Fred hasn't been feelin' so good lately, so your father took him out to the Swanson's Ointment factory and the foreman out there rubbed Old Fred down with Swanson's Ointment. Well, Old Fred stood there a minute, then he got a wild look in his eye. He whinnied, pawed the ground, jumped ten feet in the air, took off, cleared a twelve-foot brick wall, and headed out of town doin' eighty miles an hour. Your father asked the foreman how much ointment he used on Old Fred, and the foreman says about sixty cents' worth. And your father says, "You better rub about two dollars' worth on me—I got to go catch him!"

Well, son, I must close now and go help your father shovel some peanuts. He went to a White Elephant Sale and—well, you guessed it.

Love,
Mamma

Dear Pearl: *(Mamma always said I was as cute as a button.)* Things are fine in Mount Idy *(she goes on)*. We're having the big Mount Idy Harvest Festival. My, it's so colorful, especially Grandpa Ogg's nose. You've never seen such a nose, it's so red. He's the only person in Mount Idy who can cross the street against traffic without holding his hand up.

Wallace Swine is running the hot dog stand at the festival. He has a big sign over his booth that says, Dine With Swine.

Leonard Box eats all his meals there. After all, he eats like a pig, anyway.

Elsie Krack is running the kissing booth. The boys don't mind paying Elsie a nickel for a kiss, but they say it's awful tough climbing up that tree. She just got back from Europe. She came home on a banana boat. It cost her $847.00—$47.00 for her passage, and $800.00 for all the bananas she ate. When the boat docked, it didn't have any cargo. She sure loves bananas. She's the only person I know who can eat them sideways. A reporter asked Elsie why she was so crazy about bananas, and she said, "Ever since I was a little child, I've always liked to hang around with the bunch."

Well, son, I must close now and go help your father. He just tried an experiment. He filled his pipe with half tobacco and half gunpowder to see if it would light faster. It backfired.

                                  Love,
                                  Mamma

Dear Ace: *(Mamma always said I was a card.)* Things are fine in Mount Idy *(she goes on)*. Your father jest invented a new perfume, it's called Help! Every woman who buys a bottle of it is also given a chair and a whip. Irma Clodd wore some of it the other day and a policeman's horse kissed her. That's the first time Irma's ever been kissed—by anything. Ludlow Bean, the dentist, married Birdie Rodd, the manicurist, two months ago, and they've been fighting tooth and nail ever since. Birdie says she never should have married a dentist in the first place, he always looks down in the mouth. Ludlow gets pretty sore at her, too. He says every time he comes home from the office, she starts singing, "The Yanks are Coming!"

We're all so happy for Wallace Swine's oldest boy. He was an unwanted child, now that he's nineteen he's wanted in twenty-four states.

There's a rumor around Mount Idy that Byron Ogg married the Widow Darby because her husband died and left her eighty thousand dollars. Your father says he don't think Byron is that kind of boy. He says Byron would have married her, no matter who had left her the money.

Well, son, I must close now and go help your father. He went hunting yesterday and he wired a pair of antlers to his hat so he could get up closer to the deer. The first deer he ran into stood up and shot him!

                                    Love,
                                    Mamma

Dear Castor Oil: *(Mamma always said I was hard to take.)* Things are fine in Mount Idy *(she goes on).* How do you like Hollywood? Have you run into Bryant Washburn or J. Warren Kerrigan yet? They are a couple of new stars I see in the movies on television. Is Lassie really a boy? Is Rex the wild horse as wild as they say he is? They say he stays up half the night—and sleeps with his shoes on. My goodness!

Elsie Krack had to quit her job at the Mount Idy pretzel factory. She twisted so many pretzels last week she got the bends. Maybe it's best. We all hated to see her working with crooked dough.

Grandpa Ogg is very happy. For ten years he hasn't been able to hear a thing. Last Saturday he rubbed Swanson's Ointment on his ears, and today he heard from his brother in Nebraska.

Your father just got a haircut from Mr. Schultz, who used to be a butcher. I just saw it—Mr. Schultz is *still* a butcher. Your father's head looks like a pot roast. Twice this afternoon I caught him with his head in the oven. I didn't mind that so much, but he looked so silly with those carrots stuck over his ears.

Birdie Rodd dropped by yesterday, and she had on a diamond as big as a tomato. Your father says to her, "Where'd you get that?" and Birdie says, "When Grandma died, she left me three thousand dollars to buy a stone in her memory—this is the stone!"

Well, son, I must close now and go help your father. He just kissed a bride and got himself a black eye. I know everyone does it—but not seven years after the wedding.

Love,
Mamma

Dear Gorgonzola: *(Mamma always wanted me to be the big cheese.)* Things are fine in Mount Idy *(she goes on—doesn't she!).* Your father and I had a wonderful time last night. We didn't see each other all evening. He finally sneaked in at 3:00 A.M. He said he had spent the evening at Joe Cutter's Pool Hall and Supper Club. I said, "How was the floor show?" and he says, "I don't know—but they tell me I was in it!" Then I says, "Was it crowded?" and he says, "No—not under *our* table!"

Mrs. Wallace Swine dropped by last Monday with her seventeen-year-old twins. My, but they do look alike. Honestly, I can't tell Fred from Gladys. Mrs.

Swine can tell them apart. She says it's easy—all you do is stick your finger in Fred's mouth, and if he bites you, it's Gladys. Maybe that's why she always wears gloves.

Last Saturday night your father and I went to Grandma Ogg's birthday party. Grandma just had her hair fixed and she certainly didn't look eighty-two—she looked ninety-four.

We all played games at the party. First we played Spin the Bottle—after your father had emptied it. Then we played a new version of Drop the Handkerchief. Instead of a handkerchief, we used a real live person. This turned out to be lots of fun because Grandma lives on the eighth floor. Then we played Pin the Tail on the Donkey. Seven of the guests had to be rushed to the hospital. They never should have used a live donkey.

Well, son, I must close now and go help your father. He was coming up the stairs with five gallons of elderberry wine, and he slipped and fell clear down into the basement. Fortunately, he didn't spill a drop—he kept his mouth closed.

Love,
Mamma

Dear Hula Hoop: *(Mamma always said I had a way of getting around people.)* Things are fine in Mount Idy *(she goes on—and on—and on)*. Well, it's election time here and everybody is running for some kind of office. Byron Ogg ran for mayor last year, and when he quit running he was in Mexico. Ludlow Bean is the most promising candidate. He'll promise you anything. He's also the most honest man in the race. He's so honest that for the past seven years he's run the public baths at Snider's Swamp, and he's never taken *one*—at least not in public.

Your father and I are going to vote for Ludlow Bean for mayor. Your father says two heads are better than one. Not ours—Ludlow's. He has several advantages over the other candidates. He can kiss twice as many babies, smoke twice as many cigars, and talk out of both sides of both mouths at the same time. Of course if he becomes mayor he'll have to give up his present job at the Bide-a-Wee Book Store, where he is now employed as book ends. He's the only man in Mount Idy who can check his own cavities.

Grandma Ogg threw a big party last night. She was on her way home from a meeting of the girls of the Let's Give Alf Landon Another Whirl At It Club, when this big party stuck a gun in her back. As I said before, last night Grandma threw a big party. They say he may live.

Well, son, I must close now and go help your father. He found an old Civil War cannon ball and he took it and a hammer out in the back yard to see if it was still any good—it was. I'm going to tell him a thing or two when he comes down.

Love,
Mamma

Dear Santa Claus: *(Mamma always wanted me to go out with a bag on Christmas Eve.)* Things are fine in Mount Idy *(she goes on)*. Byron Ogg came into a lot of money last week by a lucky stroke. His uncle had the stroke. Your father asked him what he was going to do with the money, and Byron said he was going to buy two hundred gallons of elderberry wine, thirty-seven suits of silk underwear, and several beaver hats, and if he had any money left, he'd probably just spend that foolishly. My, I'm so glad Byron's rich. I can remember when he made his first dollar. He got seven years for making it. They never would have caught him if he hadn't put his wife's picture on it. She doesn't look anything like George Washington—she looks like Grover Cleveland, especially with her mustache and bald spot.

Leonard Box was arrested yesterday. Somebody told him his wife was as pretty as a picture, so he hung her on the wall.

Clara Kimball Moots dropped by yesterday with her new dog. She told your father it was part collie and part bull and cost $500.00. I said which part is bull, and your father says the part about the $500.00.

Well, son, I must close now and go help your father. I've been doing some alterations on one of my dresses and your father just kissed me good night before I had a chance to take the pins out of my mouth.

Love,
Mamma

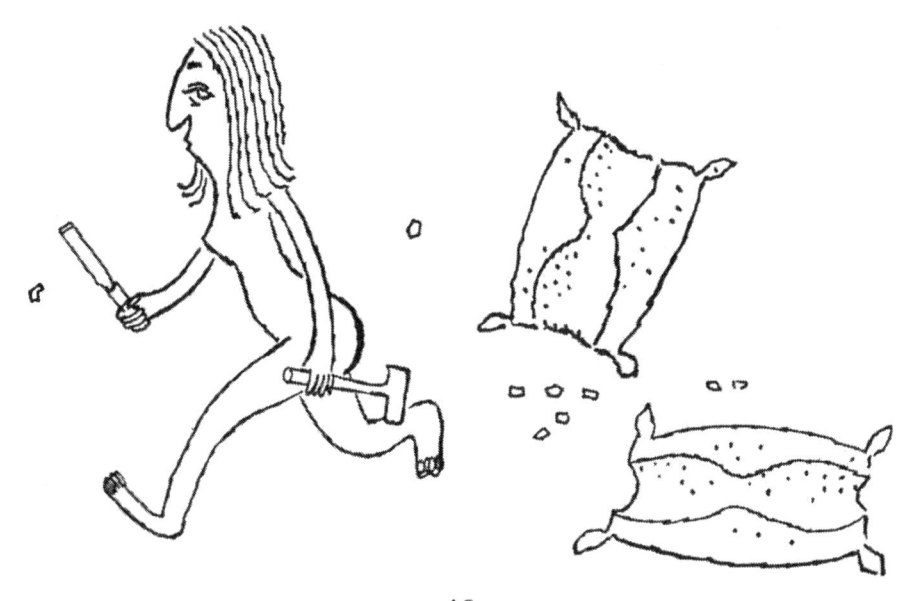

Dear Clark: *(Mamma always wanted a little gable in her house.)* Things are fine in Mount Idy *(she goes on).* Elsie Krack won a beauty contest. It happened at the Mount Idy county fair. She was looking at the hogs and a judge pinned a blue ribbon on her. This is not easy because Elsie is a nudist. My, she looks so good. Too bad muscles like that were wasted on a woman. She can bend a horseshoe right in half—with the horse still on it. My, she was so excited when she won, she kissed one of the judges and his ears disappeared. She's as strong as an ox, and on a hot day, she's even stronger. She appeared at the outdoor dance that night in a lovely sack dress. Then it rained. Too bad it was a cement sack! She had to undress that night with a hammer and chisel. She won a free trip to New York, so we all went down to the depot to see them crate her. Your father and I gave her a going-away present. A nice pair of shoes, she wears a size two and a half—two cowhides and a half a bushel of nails.

Your father and I had lots of fun at the fair. We saw one man who was selling snake oil. He said he had been using it all his life and that he was 362 years old. Your father didn't believe him, so he went up to the ticket seller and he says to him, "Has that feller really been taking that snake oil for 362 years?" And the ticket seller says, "I don't know. I only been working for him for the past 186 years!"

Well, son, I must close now and go help your father. He was standing out in the yard and a bolt of lightning knocked him flat on his back. He was standing out there again to see if lightning ever strikes twice in the same place. He's on his back again—that should answer his question.

Love,
Mamma

Dear Melba: *(Mamma always wanted me to be the toast of the town.)* Things aren't so good in Mount Idy *(she presumes).* Your father is out of work again. People just don't seem to be buying buggy whips any more. Work is hard to get in Mount Idy. Things are so bad the pigeons are feeding the people.

Elsie Krack dropped by yesterday. My, she looked lovely! She just had her hair done. She waited at our house until they sent it over. She has a nice head of skin. Your father thought she was Yul Brynner's sister. She has a number of nasty bruises on her head. Seems she was at the market near the honeydew melons and several people pinched her head. When she came in the house, she said to your father, "I've just come from the beauty parlor." And your father says, "My, it's too bad they were closed!"

Then she said to your father, "Will you drive me home?" and he says, "Yes—if you'll slip into your harness!" That didn't make her a bit mad. She just patted your father on the head—with a chair. I rushed your father to the hospital. He was very worried when they wheeled him into the operating room. He says to the doctor, "Doctor, tell me the truth. After this operation, will I be able to play the piano?" And the doctor says, "Of course you will." And your father says, "That's funny. I couldn't play it before!"

Well, son, I must close now and go help your father. The doctor's choking him to death!

                                            Love,
                                            Mamma

Dear Zero: *(Mamma always said I was nothin'.)* I was going to tell you all the news and also send you the fifty dollars I owe you, but I see I have already sealed the letter.

Love,
Mamma

Dear Nero: *(Mamma always said I fiddled around too much.)* Things are fine in Mount Idy *(she goes on).* Wallace Swine's little boy ran away from home three months ago. It took them three months to find him—they didn't look. He's the sort of little boy you don't like at first, and later you get to hate him. He always got the highest marks in school—black and blue marks on the top of his head.

Leonard Box was arrested for bringing his wife her breakfast in bed. She lives at the YWCA. It's too bad they've separated! They were such a lovely couple. She was so bowlegged and he was so knock-kneed that when they walked down the street they spelled OX. She's so bowlegged she can play a kettledrum sitting down. Leonard says when he married her she had the face of a saint—a Saint Bernard. After they were married a year, two little strangers came to bless their home—her mother and father. Leonard got along fine with her father. He was a bartender at the jail. He finally went stir-crazy making martinis. One night he came home and said to his wife, "Call the doctor! I got my nose broken in three places." And she said to him, "I told you to stay out of those places."

Well, son, I must close now and go help your father. He just went down to the barn to feed the pigs with Grandpa Ogg. There's a big fist fight going on down there. Grandpa doesn't want to be fed to the pigs.

Love,
Mamma

Dear Sun: *(Mamma always called me that, 'cause I was so bright.)* Things are fine in Mount Idy. They stopped ringing the curfew bell here at nine o'clock. It was wakin' everybody up.

Your father just invented a wonderful new plant food. It's so powerful the plants come into the house for it. He put some on a little plant the other day, and in less than five minutes we had to call the fire department to come and get him down out of the top branches.

Grandpa Ogg has been having a little trouble. Yesterday he misplaced his glasses—can't see a thing without them—so he ate a whole can of dog food by mistake. All day long today he's been chasing cars. He bit the postman twice, and there isn't a cat left in his part of town. Then this evening Grandma Ogg had to call for an ambulance. It seems that Grandpa was up on the couch tryin' to scratch a flea back of his ear with his foot, and he fell off and almost broke his neck.

The Wallace Swines have a new baby. Of course I never heard of anyone having an old baby! Ha ha! Your father and I went over to see it. It has snow-white hair—Mrs. Swine is so nearsighted she keeps putting the talcum powder on the wrong end. Your father embarrassed me so! The minute he saw the baby he said, "Wally, you should have sent him back and kept the stork."

Well, son, I must close now and go help your father. Mr. Swine just gave him a cigar—right in the eye!

Love,
Mamma

Dear Winesap: *(Mamma always called me that because I was the apple of her eye.)* Things are fine in Mount Idy. Leonard Box dropped by yesterday. My, he's getting so tall! He's growing right up through the top of his hair. He's seven feet tall now. He told your father he has to sleep in an eight-foot bed, and your father says, "That's a lot of bunk." Get it, son? Bunk bed! Ha ha!

Then Leonard said to your father, "I wouldn't talk if I was as fat as you are," and your father said, "I ain't fat. I'm just six inches too short!"

After Leonard left, your father took me to a stage show. My, they had a big orchestra and a chorus of over seventy—all except one of the girls. She was sixty-eight. During the show a man came up and said to your father, "You have my seat," and your father said, "If I had your seat I'd write to Robert L. Ripley!" Then the man looked at his ticket and he said, "I apologize, sir. I'm supposed to be in a box!" And your father said, "You keep pesterin' me and you *will* be in a box—with bronze handles on it!"

After the show, your father took me to the Mount Idy Hilton Hotel where we had dinner and danced on the roof, which wasn't easy because the roof was so steep and we didn't have our sneakers on. After the dance there were no buses or streetcars running, so I said to your father, "What will we do?" and he said, "Let's take a cab!" Which we did. I still think he should have waited until the driver returned.

Well, son, I must close now and go help your

father. They've got him in jail, and I've got to find a recipe on how to bake a three-layer cake with a hacksaw in it.

>Love,
>Mamma

Dear Honest Abe: *(Mamma wants to know my Gettysburg address.)* Things are fine in Mount Idy. Your father has a new hobby—painting in oil. He was painting an oil tank and fell in. Of course he comes by his painting talent honestly. Your grandfather was a great artist—a booze artist. He once painted a hen so realistic that when they hung the picture in the museum it laid an egg—in more ways than one. Ha ha! Your father says they should have hung Grandpa instead.

Mrs. Wallace Swine is suing Dr. Beemish for operating on her husband. She claims it's against the law to open another person's male.

Grandpa Ogg dropped in last night and he and your father spent the whole evening insulting each other. Grandpa started it. He says to your father, "Is that your nose, or are you eating a banana?" Then your father said, "I seldom forget a face, but in your case I'll make an exception." Then Grandpa got real mad and says, "Is that your lower lip, or are you wearin' a turtle-neck sweater?"

Son, I don't mind those two insulting each other, but I think your father went just a little bit too far when he and Grandpa went out in the hot sun to play Croquet and Grandpa had a stroke—and your father made him count it.

Well, son, I must close now and go help your father. He just stuck his head in the elevator shaft to see if the elevator was coming up—it was coming down.

Love,
Mamma

Dear William: *(Mamma always wanted me to be-Holden.)* Things are fine in Mount Idy *(she goes on)*. Ludlow Bean was arrested for doing his Christmas shopping too early. They caught him in the store before it was open.

Clara Kimball Moots will not be able to play Santa Claus this year. She can't get the henna out of her beard. She may portray one of the reindeer instead.

Mr. and Mrs. Wallace Swine have been fighting again. He won't give her an owl for her birthday, and she won't mend his socks. She says, "If he don't give a hoot, I don't give a darn."

Your father bought one of them new automatic milking machines for our cows. Last night he went to bed and forgot to shut off the machine. This morning all of our cows were turned wrong side out.

He says he's going to sell the machine and buy an octopus. Now that it's so cold in Mount Idy, your father can't milk the cows by hand because he has to wear his wool mittens. This tickles the cows. They get hysterical and nothing comes out but cottage cheese.

Two weeks ago your father and I went fishing. I accidentally dropped my wedding ring into the lake. I was so upset about it I cried for two weeks. Last night we had dinner at the Mount Idy Hilton, and I ordered fish. And when it came, what do you think I found in that fish—bones!

Well, son, I must close now and go help your father. He just fainted and I brought him to. Now he wants two more.

Love,
Mamma

Dear Razor: *(Mamma always said I was such a cute little shaver.)* Things are fine in Mount Idy *(she goes on).* Grandpa and Grandma Ogg's little boy has one tooth—he's seventy-two years old. He's not too bright you know. He was fifty-four years old before he learned to wave by-by! He's been in the fourth grade at school so long that last year they didn't pass him—they made him chairman of the board.

You'd hardly know Grandpa Ogg now. He's got a permanent wave in his beard. When he was washing it in a bucket of water the other night, he reached up to turn on the light and stuck his finger in an open socket. Then everything happened—his hearing aid backfired and blew the pocket out of his shirt; the nails in his shoes got red-hot, and he was arrested for going through town ninety miles an hour—without a car. His eyeglasses look like they're made of neon. He's the only person in Mount Idy who can read a book in a pitch-black room. He also gets Government time signals through a gold filling in his mouth.

Their cat sat down on a live wire and now they get all the disc jockeys through the cat. Visiting Grandpa and Grandma Ogg is like taking a tour through the electric company. Grandpa's afraid to kiss Grandma good night for fear he might plunge Mount Idy into total darkness.

Well, son, I must close now and go help your father. He just shook hands with Grandpa Ogg, and I've got to go take him a robe.

                        Love,
                        Mamma

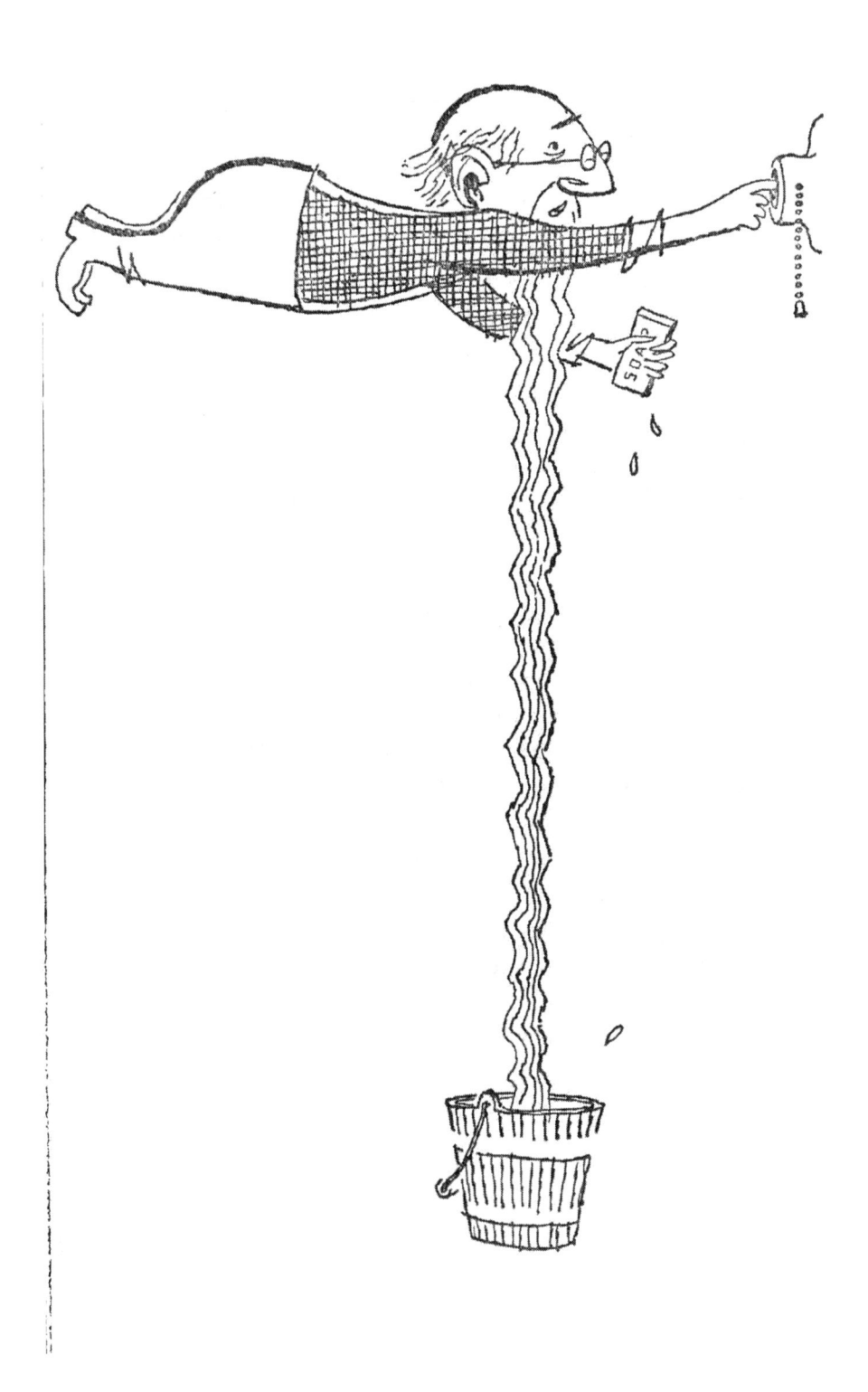
SOAP

Dear Ferris: *(Mamma always wanted me to be a big wheel.)* Things are fine in Mount Idy *(she goes on)*. I just made your father's lunch—a mother-in-law sandwich. Cold shoulder and tongue. Byron Ogg just lost his mother-in-law. Your father said to him, "It must be hard to lose a mother-in-law," and Byron says, "It's almost impossible."

Your father and I spent the evening with the Wallace Swines last night. Their little boy—Hazel —spent the whole evening pounding nails into their new furniture. Finally your father said to Mr. Swine, "How can you afford to let him do that?" And Mr. Swine says, "Oh, it's not so bad. We get the nails wholesale."

Leonard Box and his brother got up at four o'clock this morning and went hunting. They were hunting for their father. They finally found him. He had been arrested for driving twenty miles an hour. Leonard says to the judge, "You can't arrest a man for driving twenty miles an hour," and the judge said, "No? In a stolen car?" Then Leonard took $137.27 out of his pocket and paid his father's fine, and his father says, "Where did you get $137.27?" Leonard says, "I won it playing poker." And his father said, "How did you get such an odd figure?" and Leonard says, "I eat too much."

Well, son, I must close now and go help your father catch a cat. He wants to restring his tennis racket.

Love,
Mamma

Dear Sonny Boy: Things are fine here in Mount Idy. Melvin Box stopped by the house today. He had his son with him. My, he's a bright boy! He can say Da-da, Ma-ma, and wave by-by, which should help him a lot when he goes into the army next week. Reminds me of the time, in World War II, when Byron Ogg joined the WACS. All durin' the war he couldn't figure out why his outfit never shaved. Only last week his mother got him to stop wearing a girdle.

Your Grandpa Weaver came home last week on a furlough. He says with any kind of luck Grant should take Richmond this summer. What upsets me the most is: your father agrees with him.

Your Aunt Lottie and Uncle Delbert have separated. Three years ago she read *A Tale of Two Cities*, and later she had the twins. Then she heard that song, "Three Little Words," and had triplets. Then she went to the Four Star Theater and had the quadruplets. Your uncle finally left her when she told him she wanted to spend their vacation at the Thousand Islands.

                        Love,
                        Mamma

Dear Spike: *(Mamma always wanted me to be sharp as a tack.)* Things are fine in Mount Idy. Gomar Cool and Irma Clodd, the harpist, got married. He hated her, but he loves to have his back scratched. Your father said to him, "Gomar, whatever happened to that ugly, pop-eyed, buck-toothed girl you use to go with?" And Gomar said, "I married her." They get along fine, though. At first they were going to move in with *her* folks, but they had to give up that idea because her folks are still living with their folks.

Irma's face is so long she could eat oats out of a churn. When they was married, the minister said, "Do you take this—*woman!*" Gomar took his bride to the Mount Idy Hilton Hotel on their honeymoon. They had dinner in the newly-decorated Judge Crater Room. Gomar ordered vegetable soup. The waiter insisted that he have the chicken broth. Gomar argued about ten minutes with the waiter, who finally and disgustedly brought the vegetable soup. That night there was a sick guest in the room next to theirs. By mistake the doctor dashed into Gomar's room and gave him a big shot in the arm with a needle. Next day at lunch Gomar's wife wanted the vegetable soup, and Gomar said, "You'd better order the chicken broth. If you don't, they'll come up in the middle of the night and shoot it into your arm."

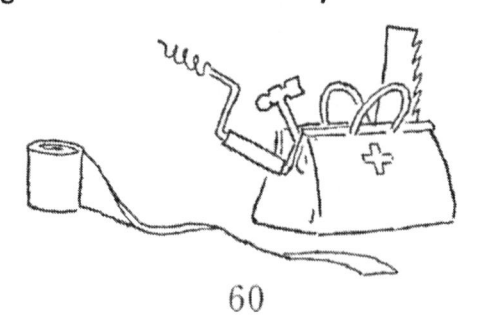

Well, son, I must close now and go help your father.. He's a tree surgeon now, and he just fell thirty-six feet out of one of his patients.

>Love,
>Mamma

About the Author

CLIFF ARQUETTE's career has spanned radio, movies, the theater, and finally television. At one time he had thirteen daily radio shows emanating from studios all over Chicago. The problem of a tight schedule was overcome by setting up an elaborate transportation schedule which included a motor boat trip on the river.

Three years ago he retired from show business, but was tempted by Jack Paar to make several guest appearances on NBC's Jack Paar Show. Ironically, these have brought him more fame and fortune than anything else in his career.

Cliff says, with a chuckle, that he developed the "Letters From Mamma" routine because ". . . I'm lazy and I don't like to memorize things. So I write myself letters to read. Easier that way."

The Library of Congress has catalogued this book as follows:

Arquette, Cliff.
 Charley Weaver's letters from mamma. Introd. by Jack Paar. Illustrated by Sidney A. Quinn with a little help from Charley. [1st ed.] Philadelphia, J. C. Winston Co. [1959]

 64 p. illus. 22 cm.

 1. American wit and humor.   i. Title.

PN6162.A67   817.54   59–9931 ‡

Library of Congress

"I'll have to talk to Mamma about that one!"

"That's what Mamma said, Johnnie."

"Birdie gets married so often she keeps her brides-maids, ushers and flower girls on salary."

THE JOHN C. WINSTON COMPANY
Philadelphia • Toronto

www.ingramcontent.com/pod-product-compliance
Lightning Source LLC
Chambersburg PA
CBHW071227100325
23261CB00010B/465